# Don't Ask **Google,**

# Ask the **Bible**

For Answers to
Life's Biggest Questions,

# Don't Ask
# **Google,**

# Ask the
# **Bible**

Compiled by
**Joe Kirby**

CLC INTERNATIONAL | Multi-Language Media
Foreign Language Christian Resources

*For Answers to Life's Biggest Questions, Don't Ask Google, Ask the Bible*

Published by Multi-Language Media, an imprint of
CLC Publications

USA: P.O. Box 1449, Fort Washington, PA 19034
www.clcpublications.com

UK: Kingsway CLC Trust
Unit 5, Glendale Avenue, Sandycroft, Flintshire, CH5 2QP
www.equippingthechurch.com

Printed in the United States of America

ISBN (paperback): 978-1-61958-335-1

# Contents

# Introduction

If you want to find out how to fix your bicycle or the words to your favorite song, Google is your best friend. The problem is, people think Google has the answer to everything else in the world, too. Sometimes when I'm speaking to an audience and telling a real-life story, someone later accuses me of making it up—because they couldn't find it on Google!

Google may have a lot of information, but it is *not* the source of all knowledge. There are still great depths of wisdom to be found in books, and there is one book that was around long before Google—and will be here long after it!

Jesus said, "Heaven and earth will pass away, but my words will not pass away" (Matthew 24:35, ESV). The Bible has an answer to every key question in life because the author of the Bible is also the author of life.

That's how this book came about. I've compiled some of the world's most-searched topics and questions on Google, and then tried to answer them, using *only* the Bible.

Why? Because the Bible isn't just your average book. It's alive! What do you do if you are lost on some obscure road in the middle of nowhere? If you have a phone with a GPS, you can find out exactly where you are. The same applies to the Bible. It can show you exactly where you are on the journey of life, and speak directly to your heart.

If you don't believe me, try reading this book for a few minutes. I'm sure God will speak to your heart in a way you were least expecting.

So turn the page and enjoy your journey! And if you have any questions about the Bible, God, or Jesus, here's a website that can help:

**www.gotquestions.org**

Joe Kirby
Off the Kirb Ministries
www.offthekirb.co.uk

# Google's Most-Searched Questions

### *What is love?*

Love is patient and kind; love does not envy or boast; it is not arrogant or rude. It does not insist on its own way; it is not irritable or resentful; it does not rejoice at wrongdoing, but rejoices with the truth. Love bears all things, believes all things, hopes all things, endures all things. Love never ends.

*1 Corinthians 13:4–8* (ESV)

Greater love has no one than this, than to lay down one's life for his friends.

*John 15:13* (NKJV)

This is love: not that we loved God, but that he loved us and sent his Son as an atoning sacrifice for our sins.

*1 John 4:10* (NIV)

### *What is the Bible?*

Every scripture is inspired by God and useful for teaching, for reproof, for correction, and for training in righteousness.

*2 Timothy 3:16* (NET)

Your word is a lamp to guide my feet and a light for my path.

*Psalm 119:105* (NLT)

For the word of God is living and active, sharper than any two-edged sword, piercing to the division of soul and of spirit, of joints and of marrow, and discerning the thoughts and intentions of the heart.

*Hebrews 4:12* (ESV)

The law of the LORD is perfect, converting the soul; The testimony of the LORD is sure, making wise the simple; The statutes of the LORD are right, rejoicing the heart; The commandment of the LORD is pure, enlightening the eyes; The fear of the LORD is clean, enduring forever; The

judgments of the LORD are true and righteous altogether.
More to be desired are they than gold, Yea, than much
fine gold; Sweeter also than honey and the honeycomb.
Moreover by them Your servant is warned, And in keeping
them there is great reward.

*Psalm 19:7–11* (NKJV)

## *What is reality?*

The Spirit of God has made me; the breath of the Almighty
gives me life.

*Job 33:4* (NIV)

But it is a spirit in people, the breath of the Almighty that
makes them understand.

*Job 32:8* (NET)

## *Who am I?*

Then God said, "Let us make human beings in our image,
to be like us. They will reign over the fish in the sea, the
birds in the sky, the livestock, all the wild animals on the
earth, and the small animals that scurry along the ground."

*Genesis 1:26* (NLT)

So God created man in his own image, in the image of God
he created him; male and female he created them.

*Genesis 1:27* (ESV)

But as many as received Him, to them He gave the right to
become children of God, to those who believe in His name.

*John 1:12* (NKJV)

Now if we are children, then we are heirs—heirs of God
and co-heirs with Christ, if indeed we share in his sufferings
in order that we may also share in his glory.

*Romans 8:17* (NIV)

I no longer call you slaves, because a master doesn't confide in his slaves. Now you are my friends, since I have told you everything the Father told me.

*John 15:15* (NLT)

## *What is the meaning of life?*

Having heard everything, I have reached this conclusion: Fear God and keep his commandments, because this is the whole duty of man.

*Ecclesiastes 12:13* (NET)

O people, the LORD has told you what is good, and this is what he requires of you: to do what is right, to love mercy, and to walk humbly with your God.

*Micah 6:8* (NLT)

And he said to them, "Take care, and be on your guard against all covetousness, for one's life does not consist in the abundance of his possessions."

*Luke 12:15* (ESV)

## *What is the fear of God?*

The fear of the LORD is the beginning of knowledge, but fools despise wisdom and instruction.

*Proverbs 1:7* (NKJV)

The fear of the LORD is the beginning of wisdom; all who follow his precepts have good understanding. To him belongs eternal praise.

*Psalm 111:10* (NIV)

Fearing the LORD leads to life, and one who does so will live satisfied; he will not be afflicted by calamity.

*Proverbs 19:23* (NET)

### *What is truth?*

Jesus told him, "I am the way, the truth, and the life. No one can come to the Father except through me."

*John 14:6* (NLT)

Then Pilate said to him, "So you are a king?" Jesus answered, "You say that I am a king. For this purpose I was born and for this purpose I have come into the world—to bear witness to the truth. Everyone who is of the truth listens to my voice."

*John 18:37* (ESV)

You shall know the truth, and the truth shall make you free.

*John 8:32* (NKJV)

As it is, you are looking for a way to kill me, a man who has told you the truth that I heard from God.

*John 8:40* (NIV)

### *What is evil?*

Dear friend, do not imitate what is bad but what is good. The one who does good is of God; the one who does what is bad has not seen God.

*3 John 1:11* (NET)

But the words you speak come from the heart—that's what defiles you.

*Matthew 15:18* (NLT)

You are of your father the devil, and your will is to do your father's desires. He was a murderer from the beginning, and does not stand in the truth, because there is no truth in him. When he lies, he speaks out of his own character, for he is a liar and the father of lies.

*John 8:44* (ESV)

Do you not know that the unrighteous will not inherit the kingdom of God? Do not be deceived. Neither fornicators, nor idolaters, nor adulterers, nor homosexuals, nor sodomites, nor thieves, nor covetous, nor drunkards, nor revilers, nor extortioners will inherit the kingdom of God. And such were some of you. But you were washed, but you were sanctified, but you were justified in the name of the Lord Jesus and by the Spirit of our God.

*1 Corinthians 6:9–11* (NKJV)

## *Is there life after death?*

Jesus said to her, "I am the resurrection and the life. The one who believes in me will live, even though they die."

*John 11:25* (NIV)

Now we do not want you to be uninformed, brothers and sisters, about those who are asleep, so that you will not grieve like the rest who have no hope. For if we believe that Jesus died and rose again, so also we believe that God will bring with him those who have fallen asleep as Christians. For we tell you this by the word of the Lord, that we who are alive, who are left until the coming of the Lord, will surely not go ahead of those who have fallen asleep. For the Lord himself will come down from heaven with a shout of command, with the voice of the archangel, and with the trumpet of God, and the dead in Christ will rise first. Then we who are alive, who are left, will be suddenly caught up together with them in the clouds to meet the Lord in the air. And so we will always be with the Lord. Therefore encourage one another with these words.

*1 Thessalonians 4:13–18* (NET)

Each person is destined to die once and after that comes judgment.

*Hebrews 9:27* (NLT)

Do not marvel at this, for an hour is coming when all who are in the tombs will hear his voice and come out, those who have done good to the resurrection of life, and those who have done evil to the resurrection of judgment.

*John 5:28–29* (ESV)

I have hope in God, which they themselves also accept, that there will be a resurrection of the dead, both of the just and the unjust.

*Acts 24:15* (NKJV)

And the dust returns to the ground it came from, and the spirit returns to God who gave it.

*Ecclesiastes 12:7* (NIV)

### What is religion?

Pure and undefiled religion before God the Father is this: to care for orphans and widows in their adversity and to keep oneself unstained by the world.

*James 1:27* (NET)

We are all infected and impure with sin. When we display our righteous deeds, they are nothing but filthy rags. Like autumn leaves, we wither and fall, and our sins sweep us away like the wind.

*Isaiah 64:6* (NLT)

Who can bring a clean thing out of an unclean? There is not one.

*Job 14:4* (ESV)

Who also made us sufficient as ministers of the new covenant, not of the letter but of the Spirit; for the letter kills, but the Spirit gives life.

*2 Corinthians 3:6* (NKJV)

Be careful not to practice your righteousness in front of others to be seen by them. If you do, you will have no reward from your Father in heaven. So when you give to the needy, do not announce it with trumpets, as the hypocrites do in the synagogues and on the streets, to be honored by others. Truly I tell you, they have received their reward in full. But when you give to the needy, do not let your left hand know what your right hand is doing, so that your giving may be in secret. Then your Father, who sees what is done in secret, will reward you. And when you pray, do not be like the hypocrites, for they love to pray standing in the synagogues and on the street corners to be seen by others. Truly I tell you, they have received their reward in full.

*Matthew 6:1–5* (NIV)

For the one who obeys the whole law but fails in one point has become guilty of all of it.

*James 2:10* (NET)

I do not treat the grace of God as meaningless. For if keeping the law could make us right with God, then there was no need for Christ to die.

*Galatians 2:21* (NLT)

### What is faith?

Now faith is the assurance of things hoped for, the conviction of things not seen.

*Hebrews 11:1* (ESV)

For by grace you have been saved through faith, and that not of yourselves; it is the gift of God, not of works, lest anyone should boast.

*Ephesians 2:8–9* (NKJV)

For we live by faith, not by sight.

*2 Corinthians 5:7* (NIV)

## *What is beauty?*

Let your beauty not be external—the braiding of hair and wearing of gold jewelry or fine clothes—but the inner person of the heart, the lasting beauty of a gentle and tranquil spirit, which is precious in God's sight.

*1 Peter 3:3–4* (NET)

Charm is deceptive, and beauty does not last; but a woman who fears the Lord will be greatly praised.

*Proverbs 31:30* (NLT)

But the LORD said to Samuel, "Do not look on his appearance or on the height of his stature, because I have rejected him. For the LORD sees not as man sees: man looks on the outward appearance, but the LORD looks on the heart."

*1 Samuel 16:7* (ESV)

Therefore we do not lose heart. Even though our outward man is perishing, yet the inward man is being renewed day by day.

*2 Corinthians 4:16* (NKJV)

## *What is mercy?*

But go and learn what this means: "I desire mercy, not sacrifice." For I have not come to call the righteous, but sinners.

*Matthew 9:13* (NIV)

Blessed be the God and Father of our Lord Jesus Christ! By his great mercy he gave us new birth into a living hope through the resurrection of Jesus Christ from the dead.

*1 Peter 1:3* (NET)

The faithful love of the LORD never ends! His mercies never cease. Great is his faithfulness; his mercies begin afresh each morning.

*Lamentations 3:22–23* (NLT)

Let us then with confidence draw near to the throne of grace, that we may receive mercy and find grace to help in time of need.

*Hebrews 4:16* (ESV)

Therefore be merciful, just as your Father also is merciful.

*Luke 6:36* (NKJV)

Mercy triumphs over judgment.

*James 2:13* (NIV)

Blessed are the merciful, for they will be shown mercy.

*Matthew 5:7* (NET)

## *Why is hope so important?*

For in this hope we were saved. Now hope that is seen is not hope. For who hopes for what he sees? But if we hope for what we do not see, we wait for it with patience.

*Romans 8:24–25* (ESV)

O LORD, you alone are my hope. I've trusted you, O LORD, from childhood.

*Psalm 71:5* (NLT)

For whatever things were written before were written for our learning, that we through the patience and comfort of the Scriptures might have hope.

*Romans 15:4* (NKJV)

Through [Jesus] we have gained access by faith into this grace in which we now stand. And we boast in the hope of the glory of God. Not only so, but we also glory in our sufferings, because we know that suffering produces perseverance; perseverance, character; and character, hope. And hope does not put us to shame, because God's love has been poured out into our hearts through the Holy Spirit, who has been given to us.

*Romans 5:2–5* (NIV)

### *What does wisdom really mean?*

But the wisdom from above is first pure, then peaceable, gentle, accommodating, full of mercy and good fruit, impartial, and not hypocritical.

*James 3:17* (NET)

Joyful is the person who finds wisdom, the one who gains understanding. For wisdom is more profitable than silver, and her wages are better than gold. Wisdom is more precious than rubies; nothing you desire can compare with her. She offers you long life in her right hand, and riches and honor in her left. She will guide you down delightful paths; all her ways are satisfying. Wisdom is a tree of life to those who embrace her; happy are those who hold her tightly.

*Proverbs 3:13–18* (NLT)

Keep hold of instruction; do not let go; guard her, for she is your life.

*Proverbs 4:13* (ESV)

Listen to counsel and receive instruction, that you may be wise in your latter days.

*Proverbs 19:20* (NKJV)

The way of fools seems right to them, but the wise listen to advice.

*Proverbs 12:15* (NIV)

Let the word of Christ dwell in you richly, teaching and exhorting one another with all wisdom, singing psalms, hymns, and spiritual songs, all with grace in your hearts to God.

*Colossians 3:16* (NET)

For the LORD grants wisdom! From his mouth come knowledge and understanding.

*Proverbs 2:6* (NLT)

## How can I find peace?

Now may the Lord of peace himself give you peace at all times in every way. The Lord be with you all.

*2 Thessalonians 3:16* (ESV)

You will keep him in perfect peace, whose mind is stayed on You, because he trusts in You.

*Isaiah 26:3* (NKJV)

Blessed are the peacemakers, for they will be called children of God.

*Matthew 5:9* (NIV)

Peace I leave with you; my peace I give to you; I do not give it to you as the world does. Do not let your hearts be distressed or lacking in courage.

*John 14:27* (NET)

In peace I will lie down and sleep, for you alone, O LORD, will keep me safe.

*Psalm 4:8* (NLT)

## Who can I trust?

Trust in the LORD with all your heart, and do not lean on your own understanding. In all your ways acknowledge him, and he will make straight your paths.

*Proverbs 3:5–6* (ESV)

Whenever I am afraid, I will trust in You. In God (I will praise His word), in God I have put my trust; I will not fear. What can flesh do to me?

*Psalm 56:3–4* (NKJV)

Commit your way to the LORD; trust in him and he will do this.

*Psalm 37:5* (NIV)

But I trust in your faithfulness. May I rejoice because of your deliverance.

*Psalm 13:5* (NET)

Oh, the joys of those who trust the LORD, who have no confidence in the proud or in those who worship idols.

*Psalm 40:4* (NLT)

And those who know your name put their trust in you, for you, O LORD, have not forsaken those who seek you.

*Psalm 9:10* (ESV)

### Does God speak to us today?

God, who at various times and in various ways spoke in time past to the fathers by the prophets, has in these last days spoken to us by His Son, whom He has appointed heir of all things, through whom also He made the worlds.

*Hebrews 1:1–2* (NKJV)

Then he said: "The God of our ancestors has chosen you to know his will and to see the Righteous One and to hear words from his mouth."

*Acts 22:14* (NIV)

Dear friends, do not believe every spirit, but test the spirits to determine if they are from God, because many false prophets have gone out into the world.

*1 John 4:1* (NET)

Above all, you must realize that no prophecy in Scripture ever came from the prophet's own understanding, or from human initiative. No, those prophets were moved by the Holy Spirit, and they spoke from God.

*2 Peter 1:20–21* (NLT)

# Who Is God?

God is very different from us. In fact, God himself says, "For my thoughts are not your thoughts, neither are your ways my ways, declares the LORD" (Isaiah 55:8, ESV).

People usually have only a few attributes; some people are creative, others are sensitive; still others are very athletic or very analytical. It's very rare, if not impossible, for one person to have all these attributes and more.

But God is different. He has many attributes, and as a perfect, infinite spiritual being, He is consistent in all His varied attributes, even when those attributes seem to contradict each other. That explains why some people look at the Bible and say, "The God of the Old Testament isn't the same as the God of the New Testament." But God never changes, and neither does His Son, Jesus Christ: "Jesus Christ is the same yesterday and today and forever" (Hebrews 13:8, ESV).

In the Old Testament you will find just as much compassion and love as in the New. Moreover, in the New Testament you will find just as much judgment and wrath as in the Old. God is consistent, and when we say "God is love," that is true, but we must not forget His other characteristics that are also operating at the same time.

For instance, God is just; He must punish sin and injustice. But He is also loving and merciful, which is why He sent Jesus to die for our sins. At the cross, both of God's attributes of love and justice were demonstrated when Jesus was crucified. He shows His love by granting mercy to all people who are willing to turn to Him for forgiveness through Jesus' act of love on the cross. He shows His justice by punishing Jesus for our sins, so our sins are dealt with and not just brushed under the carpet. God is wonderful and I hope the verses below will give you a taste of just how vast He is, but at the same time you will understand that He desires to enter into a friendship with you and me.

### God is real

For every house is built by someone, but the builder of all things is God.

*Hebrews 3:4* (ESV)

The heavens declare the glory of God; and the firmament shows His handiwork.

*Psalm 19:1* (NKJV)

And without faith it is impossible to please God, because anyone who comes to him must believe that he exists and that he rewards those who earnestly seek him.

*Hebrews 11:6* (NIV)

Where were you when I laid the foundation of the earth? Tell me, if you possess understanding.

*Job 38:4* (NET)

### God is Creator

In the beginning God created the heavens and the earth.

*Genesis 1:1* (NLT)

By faith we understand that the universe was created by the word of God, so that what is seen was not made out of things that are visible.

*Hebrews 11:3* (ESV)

For since the creation of the world His invisible attributes are clearly seen, being understood by the things that are made, even His eternal power and Godhead, so that they are without excuse.

*Romans 1:20* (NKJV)

### God is eternal

Do you not know? Have you not heard? The LORD is the everlasting God, the Creator of the ends of the earth. He will not grow tired or weary, and his understanding no one can fathom.

*Isaiah 40:28* (NIV)

"I am the Alpha and the Omega," says the Lord God—the one who is, and who was, and who is still to come—the All-Powerful!

*Revelation 1:8* (NET)

But the LORD is the only true God. He is the living God and the everlasting King! The whole earth trembles at his anger. The nations cannot stand up to his wrath.

*Jeremiah 10:10* (NLT)

Trust in the LORD forever, for the LORD GOD is an everlasting rock.

*Isaiah 26:4* (ESV)

## God is powerful

Great is our LORD, and mighty in power; His understanding is infinite.

*Psalm 147:5* (NKJV)

By the word of the LORD the heavens were made, their starry host by the breath of his mouth.

*Psalm 33:6* (NIV)

The LORD is the one who by his power made the earth. He is the one who by his wisdom established the world. And by his understanding he spread out the skies.

*Jeremiah 10:12* (NET)

## God is good

Taste and see that the LORD is good. Oh, the joys of those who take refuge in him!

*Psalm 34:8* (NLT)

The LORD is good, a stronghold in the day of trouble; he knows those who take refuge in him.

*Nahum 1:7* (ESV)

Oh, how abundant is your goodness, which you have stored up for those who fear you and worked for those who take refuge in you, in the sight of the children of mankind!

*Psalm 31:19* (ESV)

Surely your goodness and unfailing love will pursue me all the days of my life, and I will live in the house of the LORD forever.

*Psalm 23:6* (NLT)

### God is holy

"For My thoughts are not your thoughts, nor are your ways My ways," says the LORD.

*Isaiah 55:8* (NKJV)

There is no one holy like the LORD; there is no one besides you; there is no Rock like our God.

*1 Samuel 2:2* (NIV)

For this is what the high and exalted one says, the one who rules forever, whose name is holy: "I dwell in an exalted and holy place, but also with the discouraged and humiliated, in order to cheer up the humiliated and to encourage the discouraged."

*Isaiah 57:15* (NET)

Who is like you among the gods, O LORD—glorious in holiness, awesome in splendor, performing great wonders?

*Exodus 15:11* (NLT)

### God is love

But God shows his love for us in that while we were still sinners, Christ died for us.

*Romans 5:8* (ESV)

Greater love has no one than this, than to lay down one's life for his friends.

*John 15:13* (NKJV)

And so we know and rely on the love God has for us. God is love. Whoever lives in love lives in God, and God in them.

*1 John 4:16* (NIV)

### *God is just*

As for the Rock, his work is perfect, for all his ways are just. He is a reliable God who is never unjust, he is fair and upright.

*Deuteronomy 32:4* (NET)

God alone, who gave the law, is the Judge. He alone has the power to save or to destroy. So what right do you have to judge your neighbor?

*James 4:12* (NLT)

Shall not the Judge of all the earth do what is just?

*Genesis 18:25* (ESV)

For we must all appear before the judgment seat of Christ, that each one may receive the things done in the body, according to what he has done, whether good or bad.

*2 Corinthians 5:10* (NKJV)

Nothing in all creation is hidden from God's sight. Everything is uncovered and laid bare before the eyes of him to whom we must give account.

*Hebrews 4:13* (NIV)

### *God is perfect*

Now this is the gospel message we have heard from him and announce to you: God is light, and in him there is no darkness at all.

*1 John 1:5* (NET)

God's way is perfect. All the LORD's promises prove true. He is a shield for all who look to him for protection.

*Psalm 18:30* (NLT)

You therefore must be perfect, as your heavenly Father is perfect.

*Matthew 5:48* (ESV)

### God is Spirit

God is Spirit, and those who worship Him must worship in spirit and truth.

*John 4:24* (NKJV)

The Spirit gives life; the flesh counts for nothing. The words I have spoken to you—they are full of the Spirit and life.

*John 6:63* (NIV)

Now the earth was without shape and empty, and darkness was over the surface of the watery deep, but the Spirit of God was moving over the surface of the water.

*Genesis 1:2* (NET)

No one has ever seen God. But the unique One, who is himself God, is near to the Father's heart. He has revealed God to us.

*John 1:18* (NLT)

# Let's Talk about Sin . . .

What is sin? It's the breaking of God's law. To put it vividly, it means "to miss the target." Even NBA players miss three-pointers sometimes, and no archer, even in the Olympics, hits the bullseye every time.

In the same way, it doesn't matter how hard we try, we also miss the target, because we are sinners. We tell lies, gossip, envy others, lose our tempers, and sometimes look at things we shouldn't. We break God's laws every day, just like a criminal. Because we've commited crimes against God, we don't deserve to go to heaven.

You may think, "I'm no criminal; I'm a good person," but compared to God's standard, we all stand condemned. His standard is perfection, and none of us reaches it.

You may also be thinking, "That sounds harsh; no one is perfect!" But imagine if God let the standards slip for heaven. What if He allowed liars into heaven, thieves, crude talkers, and those with wandering eyes? We would ruin heaven, just as we have done to earth.

Would you let someone enter a spotlessly clean house with even a speck of dirt on their shoe? Likewise, God cannot allow a speck of sin into His perfect heaven. So how do people get into heaven? They need to be cleaned. The good news is, Jesus can make you clean. His blood on the cross can scrub away our filthy stains, wash away our past, and remove our sins far away. Have you come to realize you're a sinner? Will you consider turning away from sin and asking Jesus to wash you clean from it?

### Is lying really that bad?

There are six things that the LORD hates, seven that are an abomination to him: haughty eyes, a lying tongue, and hands that shed innocent blood, a heart that devises wicked plans, feet that make haste to run to evil, a false witness who breathes out lies, and one who sows discord among brothers.

*Proverbs 6:16–19* (ESV)

Lying lips are an abomination to the LORD, but those who deal truthfully are His delight.

*Proverbs 12:22* (NKJV)

No one who practices deceit will dwell in my house; no one who speaks falsely will stand in my presence.

*Psalm 101:7* (NIV)

But as for the cowards, unbelievers, detestable persons, murderers, the sexually immoral, and those who practice magic spells, idol worshipers, and all those who lie, their place will be in the lake that burns with fire and sulfur. That is the second death.

*Revelation 21:8* (NET)

### Is lust really that bad?

But I say, anyone who even looks at a woman with lust has already committed adultery with her in his heart.

*Matthew 5:28* (NLT)

Flee from sexual immorality. Every other sin a person commits is outside the body, but the sexually immoral person sins against his own body.

*1 Corinthians 6:18* (ESV)

But each one is tempted when he is drawn away by his own desires and enticed. Then, when desire has conceived, it gives birth to sin; and sin, when it is full-grown, brings forth death.

*James 1:14–15* (NKJV)

Death and Destruction are never satisfied, and neither are human eyes.

*Proverbs 27:20* (NIV)

### Is anger really that bad?

But I say to you that anyone who is angry with a brother will be subjected to judgment. And whoever insults a brother will be brought before the council, and whoever says "Fool" will be sent to fiery hell.

*Matthew 5:22* (NET)

People with understanding control their anger; a hot temper shows great foolishness.

*Proverbs 14:29* (NLT)

For the anger of man does not produce the righteousness of God.

*James 1:20* (ESV)

Do not hasten in your spirit to be angry, for anger rests in the bosom of fools.

*Ecclesiastes 7:9* (NKJV)

But now you must also rid yourselves of all such things as these: anger, rage, malice, slander, and filthy language from your lips.

*Colossians 3:8* (NIV)

### Is being proud really that bad?

The wicked man is so arrogant he always thinks, "God won't hold me accountable; he doesn't care."

*Psalm 10:4* (NET)

Pride goes before destruction, and haughtiness before a fall.

*Proverbs 16:18* (NLT)

Everyone who is arrogant in heart is an abomination to the LORD; be assured, he will not go unpunished.

*Proverbs 16:5* (ESV)

When pride comes, then comes shame; But with the humble is wisdom.

*Proverbs 11:2* (NKJV)

Pride brings a person low, but the lowly in spirit gain honor.

*Proverbs 29:23* (NIV)

The fear of the LORD is to hate evil; I hate arrogant pride and the evil way and perverse utterances.

*Proverbs 8:13* (NET)

For the world offers only a craving for physical pleasure, a craving for everything we see, and pride in our achievements and possessions. These are not from the Father, but are from this world.

*1 John 2:16* (NLT)

### Is blaspheming God's name really that bad?

You shall not take the name of the LORD your God in vain, for the Lord will not hold him guiltless who takes his name in vain.

*Exodus 20:7* (ESV)

And anyone who speaks a word against the Son of Man, it will be forgiven him; but to him who blasphemes against the Holy Spirit, it will not be forgiven.

*Luke 12:10* (NKJV)

Above all, my brothers and sisters, do not swear—not by heaven or by earth or by anything else. All you need to say is a simple "Yes" or "No." Otherwise you will be condemned.

*James 5:12* (NIV)

### *Is sin really that bad?*

So whoever knows what is good to do and does not do it is guilty of sin.

*James 4:17* (NET)

Temptation comes from our own desires, which entice us and drag us away. These desires give birth to sinful actions. And when sin is allowed to grow, it gives birth to death.

*James 1:14–15* (NLT)

And he said, "What comes out of a person is what defiles him. For from within, out of the heart of man, come evil thoughts, sexual immorality, theft, murder, adultery, coveting, wickedness, deceit, sensuality, envy, slander, pride, foolishness. All these evil things come from within, and they defile a person."

*Mark 7:20–23* (ESV)

Now the works of the flesh are evident: sexual immorality, impurity, sensuality, idolatry, sorcery, enmity, strife, jealousy, fits of anger, rivalries, dissensions, divisions, envy, drunkenness, orgies, and things like these. I warn you, as I warned you before, that those who do such things will not inherit the kingdom of God.

*Galatians 5:19–21* (ESV)

If you do well, will you not be accepted? And if you do not do well, sin lies at the door. And its desire is for you, but you should rule over it.

*Genesis 4:7* (NKJV)

Surely I was sinful at birth, sinful from the time my mother conceived me.

*Psalm 51:5* (NIV)

# Who Is Jesus?

Jesus is the most beautiful person in the world. He is God yet human. He is eternal, yet one day His spirit stepped into a human body and was born of a virgin. He is co-equal with the Father, yet came into this world to serve us. He is infinitely rich, yet for our sakes became poor. He is a powerful King, yet washed His disciple's feet. He is totally perfect—there is no sin in Christ—yet He suffered the most cruel death, the death of a criminal. But perhaps above all, Jesus is the Savior of the world. We have no other hope besides Him. He was our substitute, absorbing the wrath of God for our wrongdoing. He stood in our place of condemnation as an act of love to save us. Many "saviors" today sadly die trying to rescue others; Jesus also died to rescue us. But He did not remain dead. After being buried in a tomb, on the third day He rose from the dead, showing that He was stronger than the powers of sin and death. We can share in His victory if we put our trust in Him.

Muhammad is dead, Buddha is dead, Gandhi is dead, Aristotle is dead, Michael Jackson is dead—but Jesus is alive. There is no other person that has conquered the grave and there is no other person worthy of trusting your life to—only Jesus Christ. Jesus is coming back to judge the living and the dead; one day every eye will see Him, whether they believed in Him or not. I wonder: are you ready to meet the Son of God?

## *The birth of Christ*

Now the Word became flesh and took up residence among us. We saw his glory—the glory of the one and only, full of grace and truth, who came from the Father.

*John 1:14* (NET)

The LORD himself will give you the sign. Look! The virgin will conceive a child! She will give birth to a son and will call him Immanuel (which means "God is with us").

*Isaiah 7:14* (NLT)

He is the image of the invisible God, the firstborn of all creation.

*Colossians 1:15* (ESV)

And the angel answered and said to her, "The Holy Spirit will come upon you, and the power of the Highest will overshadow you; therefore, also, that Holy One who is to be born will be called the Son of God."

*Luke 1:35* (NKJV)

Beyond all question, the mystery from which true godliness springs is great: He appeared in the flesh, was vindicated by the Spirit, was seen by angels, was preached among the nations, was believed on in the world, was taken up in glory.

*1 Timothy 3:16* (NIV)

## The deity of Christ

For in him all the fullness of deity lives in bodily form.

*Colossians 2:9* (NET)

For through him God created everything in the heavenly realms and on earth. He made the things we can see and the things we can't see—such as thrones, kingdoms, rulers, and authorities in the unseen world. Everything was created through him and for him.

*Colossians 1:16* (NLT)

And we know that the Son of God has come and has given us understanding, so that we may know him who is true; and we are in him who is true, in his Son Jesus Christ. He is the true God and eternal life.

*1 John 5:20* (ESV)

For unto us a Child is born, unto us a Son is given; and the government will be upon His shoulder. And His name will be called Wonderful, Counselor, Mighty God, Everlasting Father, Prince of Peace.

*Isaiah 9:6* (NKJV)

The Son is the radiance of God's glory and the exact representation of his being, sustaining all things by his powerful word. After he had provided purification for sins, he sat down at the right hand of the Majesty in heaven.

*Hebrews 1:3* (NIV)

Thomas replied to him, "My Lord and my God!"

*John 20:28* (NET)

[Jesus speaking] "The Father and I are one."

*John 10:30* (NLT)

All things were made through him, and without him was not any thing made that was made.

*John 1:3* (ESV)

No one has ascended to heaven but He who came down from heaven, that is, the Son of Man who is in heaven.

*John 3:13* (NKJV)

## *The mediation of Christ*

For there is one God and one mediator between God and mankind, the man Christ Jesus,

*1 Timothy 2:5* (NIV)

And so he is the mediator of a new covenant, so that those who are called may receive the eternal inheritance he has promised, since he died to set them free from the violations committed under the first covenant.

*Hebrews 9:15* (NET)

Because God's children are human beings—made of flesh and blood—the Son also became flesh and blood. For only as a human being could he die, and only by dying could he break the power of the devil, who had the power of death.

*Hebrews 2:14* (NLT)

## *The claims of Christ*

For he was teaching his disciples, saying to them, "The Son of Man is going to be delivered into the hands of men, and they will kill him. And when he is killed, after three days he will rise."

*Mark 9:31* (ESV)

I and My Father are one.

*John 10:30* (NKJV)

In the beginning was the Word, and the Word was with God, and the Word was God.

*John 1:1* (NIV)

Jesus replied, "I am the way, and the truth, and the life. No one comes to the Father except through me."

*John 14:6* (NET)

## *The death of Christ*

I am the living one. I died, but look—I am alive forever and ever! And I hold the keys of death and the grave.

*Revelation 1:18* (NLT)

But we see him who for a little while was made lower than the angels, namely Jesus, crowned with glory and honor because of the suffering of death, so that by the grace of God he might taste death for everyone.

*Hebrews 2:9* (ESV)

He who did not spare His own Son, but delivered Him up for us all, how shall He not with Him also freely give us all things?

*Romans 8:32* (NKJV)

When they came to the place called the Skull, they crucified him there, along with the criminals—one on his right, the other on his left.

*Luke 23:33* (NIV)

When he had received the sour wine, Jesus said, "It is completed!" Then he bowed his head and gave up his spirit.

*John 19:30* (NET)

He had done no wrong and had never deceived anyone. But he was buried like a criminal; he was put in a rich man's grave. But it was the LORD's good plan to crush him and cause him grief. Yet when his life is made an offering for sin, he will have many descendants. He will enjoy a long life, and the LORD's good plan will prosper in his hands.

*Isaiah 53:9–10* (NLT)

I gave my back to those who strike, and my cheeks to those who pull out the beard; I hid not my face from disgrace and spitting.

*Isaiah 50:6* (ESV)

### The substitution of Christ

All we like sheep have gone astray; we have turned, every one, to his own way; and the LORD has laid on Him the iniquity of us all.

*Isaiah 53:6* (NKJV)

Fixing our eyes on Jesus, the pioneer and perfecter of faith. For the joy set before him he endured the cross, scorning its shame, and sat down at the right hand of the throne of God.

*Hebrews 12:2* (NIV)

On the next day John saw Jesus coming toward him and said, "Look, the Lamb of God who takes away the sin of the world!"

*John 1:29* (NET)

Christ suffered for our sins once for all time. He never sinned, but he died for sinners to bring you safely home to God. He suffered physical death, but he was raised to life in the Spirit.

*1 Peter 3:18* (NLT)

But he was pierced for our transgressions; he was crushed for our iniquities; upon him was the chastisement that brought us peace, and with his wounds we are healed.

*Isaiah 53:5* (ESV)

## *The resurrection of Christ*

Jesus said to her, "I am the resurrection and the life. He who believes in Me, though he may die, he shall live."

*John 11:25* (NKJV)

For we believe that Jesus died and rose again, and so we believe that God will bring with Jesus those who have fallen asleep in him.

*1 Thessalonians 4:14* (NIV)

You killed the Originator of life, whom God raised from the dead. To this fact we are witnesses!

*Acts 3:15* (NET)

He isn't here! He is risen from the dead! Remember what he told you back in Galilee, that the Son of Man must be betrayed into the hands of sinful men and be crucified, and that he would rise again on the third day.

*Luke 24:6–7* (NLT)

Now if we have died with Christ, we believe that we will also live with him. We know that Christ, being raised from the dead, will never die again; death no longer has dominion over him. For the death he died he died to sin, once for all, but the life he lives he lives to God. So you also must consider yourselves dead to sin and alive to God in Christ Jesus.

*Romans 6:8–11* (ESV)

For to this end Christ died and rose and lived again, that He might be Lord of both the dead and the living.

*Romans 14:9* (NKJV)

## *The return of Christ*

Christ was sacrificed once to take away the sins of many; and he will appear a second time, not to bear sin, but to bring salvation to those who are waiting for him.

*Hebrews 9:28* (NIV)

For the Lord himself will come down from heaven with a shout of command, with the voice of the archangel, and with the trumpet of God, and the dead in Christ will rise first. Then we who are alive, who are left, will be suddenly caught up together with them in the clouds to meet the Lord in the air. And so we will always be with the Lord.

*1 Thessalonians 4:16–17* (NET)

Look! He comes with the clouds of heaven. And everyone will see him—even those who pierced him. And all the nations of the world will mourn for him. Yes! Amen!

*Revelation 1:7* (NLT)

But concerning that day and hour no one knows, not even the angels of heaven, nor the Son, but the Father only.

*Matthew 24:36* (ESV)

Therefore you also be ready, for the Son of Man is coming at an hour you do not expect.

*Matthew 24:44* (NKJV)

# How Do I Become a Christian?

The number of verses below may seem overwhelming. It may look like you need to "do" many things to become a Christian. But in fact, there is *nothing* you need to do—Jesus did it all when He died on the cross. Although salvation is a mystery, it is also incredibly easy to understand, so easy even a child can grasp it. It's famously been said that becoming a Christian "is as easy as ABC":

**A—Admit** that you're a sinner. As we've already seen, we've all broken God's laws and need forgiveness for our sins—otherwise we will remain separated from Him. Sin is the reason why we have lost fellowship with the God who created us.

**B—Believe** that Jesus is God's Son, the only person who can save you. He alone took the wrath of God on the cross and paid the price for your sin. He alone can cancel your debts of wrongdoing. He alone is the one who has risen from the dead and offers eternal life to all who will accept Him as Lord and Savior.

**C—Come** as you are and receive the forgiveness of sins that Jesus offers to all who will humble themselves. Come to Christ with all your baggage and sin and ask Him to transform your life.

When we come to Jesus in faith and are willing to leave behind our old life of sin to follow and obey Him, the Bible calls that *repentance*. Once a person truly believes in Christ as their Savior and makes the decision to repent by turning away from their past life of sin for a new life with Him, that is the moment a person becomes a Christian.

### *You need to hear the gospel (good news)*

But the angel said to them, "Do not be afraid. I bring you good news that will cause great joy for all the people."

*Luke 2:10* (NIV)

Now I want to make clear for you, brothers and sisters, the gospel that I preached to you, that you received and on which you stand, and by which you are being saved, if you hold firmly to the message I preached to you—unless you believed in vain. For I passed on to you as of first importance what I also received—that Christ died for our sins according to the scriptures, and that he was buried, and that he was raised on the third day according to the scriptures.

*1 Corinthians 15:1–4* (NET)

Yet it was our weaknesses he carried; it was our sorrows that weighed him down. And we thought his troubles were a punishment from God, a punishment for his own sins! But he was pierced for our rebellion, crushed for our sins. He was beaten so we could be whole. He was whipped so we could be healed.

*Isaiah 53:4–5* (NLT)

The saying is trustworthy and deserving of full acceptance, that Christ Jesus came into the world to save sinners, of whom I am the foremost.

*1 Timothy 1:15* (ESV)

You are worthy to take the scroll, and to open its seals; for You were slain, and have redeemed us to God by Your blood out of every tribe and tongue and people and nation.

*Revelation 5:9* (NKJV)

### You need to believe

They replied, "Believe in the Lord Jesus, and you will be saved—you and your household."

*Acts 16:31* (NIV)

If you confess with your mouth that Jesus is Lord and believe in your heart that God raised him from the dead, you will be saved.

*Romans 10:9* (NET)

For this is how God loved the world: He gave his one and only Son, so that everyone who believes in him will not perish but have eternal life.

*John 3:16* (NLT)

I have been crucified with Christ. It is no longer I who live, but Christ who lives in me. And the life I now live in the flesh I live by faith in the Son of God, who loved me and gave himself for me.

*Galatians 2:20* (ESV)

These [words] are written that you may believe that Jesus is the Christ, the Son of God, and that believing you may have life in His name.

*John 20:31* (NKJV)


### You need to confess

If we confess our sins, he is faithful and just and will forgive us our sins and purify us from all unrighteousness.

*1 John 1:9* (NIV)

People who conceal their sins will not prosper, but if they confess and turn from them, they will receive mercy.

*Proverbs 28:13* (NLT)

The tax collector, however, stood far off and would not even look up to heaven, but beat his breast and said, "God, be merciful to me, sinner that I am!"

*Luke 18:13* (NET)

I acknowledged my sin to you, and I did not cover my iniquity; I said, "I will confess my transgressions to the LORD," and you forgave the iniquity of my sin.

*Psalm 32:5* (ESV)

## *You need forgiveness*

Purge me with hyssop, and I shall be clean; wash me, and I shall be whiter than snow.

*Psalm 51:7* (NKJV)

"Come now, let us settle the matter," says the LORD. "Though your sins are like scarlet, they shall be as white as snow; though they are red as crimson, they shall be like wool."

*Isaiah 1:18* (NIV)

Yet the LORD our God is compassionate and forgiving, even though we have rebelled against him.

*Daniel 9:9* (NET)

In fact, according to the law of Moses, nearly everything was purified with blood. For without the shedding of blood, there is no forgiveness.

*Hebrews 9:22* (NLT)

## *You need to be born again*

Jesus answered him, "Truly, truly, I say to you, unless one is born again he cannot see the kingdom of God."

*John 3:3* (ESV)

Therefore, if anyone is in Christ, he is a new creation; old things have passed away; behold, all things have become new.

*2 Corinthians 5:17* (NKJV)

All those the Father gives me will come to me, and whoever comes to me I will never drive away.

*John 6:37* (NIV)

### *You need to receive eternal life*

And this is the way to have eternal life—to know you, the only true God, and Jesus Christ, the one you sent to earth.

*John 17:3* (NLT)

Truly, truly, I say to you, whoever hears my word and believes him who sent me has eternal life. He does not come into judgment, but has passed from death to life.

*John 5:24* (ESV)

The one who believes in the Son has eternal life. The one who rejects the Son will not see life, but God's wrath remains on him.

*John 3:36* (NET)

### *You need redemption*

In Him we have redemption through His blood, the forgiveness of sins, according to the riches of His grace.

*Ephesians 1:7* (NKJV)

Who gave himself for us to redeem us from all wickedness and to purify for himself a people that are his very own, eager to do what is good.

*Titus 2:14* (NIV)

And through him to reconcile all things to himself by making peace through the blood of his cross—through

42

him, whether things on earth or things in heaven. And you were at one time strangers and enemies in your minds as expressed through your evil deeds, but now he has reconciled you by his physical body through death to present you holy, without blemish, and blameless before him.

*Colossians 1:20–22* (NET)

For you know that God paid a ransom to save you from the empty life you inherited from your ancestors. And it was not paid with mere gold or silver, which lose their value. It was the precious blood of Christ, the sinless, spotless Lamb of God.

*1 Peter 1:18–19* (NLT)

### *You need repentance (to turn from wrongdoing)*

Repent therefore, and turn back, that your sins may be blotted out.

*Acts 3:19* (ESV)

The Lord is not slack concerning His promise, as some count slackness, but is longsuffering toward us, not willing that any should perish but that all should come to repentance.

*2 Peter 3:9* (NKJV)

But unless you repent, you too will all perish.

*Luke 13:3* (NIV)

Peter said to them, "Repent, and each one of you be baptized in the name of Jesus Christ for the forgiveness of your sins, and you will receive the gift of the Holy Spirit.

*Acts 2:38* (NET)

God overlooked people's ignorance about these things in earlier times, but now he commands everyone everywhere to repent of their sins and turn to him.

*Acts 17:30* (NLT)

If my people who are called by my name humble them-selves, and pray and seek my face and turn from their wicked ways, then I will hear from heaven and will forgive their sin and heal their land.

*2 Chronicles 7:14* (ESV)

### *You need to come to the cross*

For the message of the cross is foolishness to those who are perishing, but to us who are being saved it is the power of God.

*1 Corinthians 1:18* (NKJV)

In your relationships with one another, have the same mindset as Christ Jesus: Who, being in very nature God, did not consider equality with God something to be used to his own advantage; rather, he made himself nothing by taking the very nature of a servant, being made in human likeness. And being found in appearance as a man, he humbled himself by becoming obedient to death—even death on a cross! Therefore God exalted him to the highest place and gave him the name that is above every name.

*Philippians 2:5–9* (NIV)

He has destroyed what was against us, a certificate of indebtedness expressed in decrees opposed to us. He has taken it away by nailing it to the cross.

*Colossians 2:14* (NET)

Then, calling the crowd to join his disciples, he said, "If any of you wants to be my follower, you must give up your own way, take up your cross, and follow me."

*Mark 8:34* (NLT)

But far be it from me to boast except in the cross of our Lord Jesus Christ, by which the world has been crucified to me, and I to the world.

*Galatians 6:14* (ESV)

### *You need Christ's righteousness*

For I tell you, unless your righteousness exceeds that of the scribes and Pharisees, you will never enter the kingdom of heaven.

*Matthew 5:20* (ESV)

For Christ is the end of the law, with the result that there is righteousness for everyone who believes.

*Romans 10:4* (NET)

For He made Him who knew no sin to be sin for us, that we might become the righteousness of God in Him.

*2 Corinthians 5:21* (NKJV)

"He himself bore our sins" in his body on the cross, so that we might die to sins and live for righteousness; "by his wounds you have been healed."

*1 Peter 2:24* (NIV)

And be found in him, not because I have my own righteousness derived from the law, but because I have the righteousness that comes by way of Christ's faithfulness—a righteousness from God that is in fact based on Christ's faithfulness.

*Philippians 3:9* (NET)

Put on the new self, created after the likeness of God in true righteousness and holiness.

*Ephesians 4:24* (ESV)

# What Does the Holy Spirit Do?

The Bible is very clear that there is one God who exists in three distinct persons: God the Father, the source of all life in this world; God the Son, Jesus Christ, the Savior of the world; and God the Holy Spirit, the person we are going to consider right now.

The Holy Spirit is also a divine person who is sensitive in His character and is grieved by sin. When a person becomes a Christian, the Holy Spirit comes and lives inside that person; their body becomes His home and temple.

One of the greatest mysteries of the Christian faith is that when a person becomes a follower of Christ, God comes and lives inside that person and turns their life upside down. Just as it is impossible to be hit by a thirty-ton truck and remain unchanged, it is impossible to have the Spirit of God inside you and not be changed.

The Holy Spirit gives the Christian a new heart and new desires. For instance, the Bible, which at one time may have seemed so boring, is now the greatest page-turner. The local evangelical church, which you avoided like the plague, has now become your favorite place in the world. The Jesus you thought was for the faint-hearted has now melted your heart, and you long to know more about Him. Below are some other key roles that the Holy Spirit plays in a Christian's life.

### He convicts

And when he [the Spirit] comes, he will convict the world concerning sin and righteousness and judgment.

*John 16:8* (ESV)

Therefore, as the Holy Spirit says: "Today, if you will hear His voice, Do not harden your hearts."

*Hebrews 3:7–8* (NKJV)

### He helps

But the Advocate, the Holy Spirit, whom the Father will send in my name, will teach you all things and will remind you of everything I have said to you.

*John 14:26* (NIV)

And the Holy Spirit helps us in our weakness. For example, we don't know what God wants us to pray for. But the Holy Spirit prays for us with groanings that cannot be expressed in words. And the Father who knows all hearts knows what the Spirit is saying, for the Spirit pleads for us believers in harmony with God's own will.

*Romans 8:26–27* (NLT)

### He searches

God has revealed these to us by the Spirit. For the Spirit searches all things, even the deep things of God.

*1 Corinthians 2:10* (NET)

I am he who searches mind and heart, and I will give to each of you according to your works. . . . He who has an ear, let him hear what the Spirit says to the churches.

*Revelation 2:23, 29* (ESV)

### He empowers

I say then: Walk in the Spirit, and you shall not fulfill the lust of the flesh.

*Galatians 5:16* (NKJV)

For those who are led by the Spirit of God are the children of God.

*Romans 8:14* (NIV)

So Samuel took the horn full of olive oil and anointed him in the presence of his brothers. The Spirit of the LORD rushed upon David from that day onward. Then Samuel got up and went to Ramah.

*1 Samuel 16:13* (NET)

Then Jesus returned to Galilee, filled with the Holy Spirit's power. Reports about him spread quickly through the whole region.

*Luke 4:14* (NLT)

### He bears fruit

But the fruit of the Spirit is love, joy, peace, longsuffering, kindness, goodness, faithfulness, gentleness, self-control. Against such there is no law.

*Galatians 5:22–23* (NKJV)

For to set the mind on the flesh is death, but to set the mind on the Spirit is life and peace.

*Romans 8:6* (ESV)

# When You Need Help with Life

Life is hard. We live in a broken world, cursed by the effects of our sin, and until God comes to renew this world, each of us will face trials and problems. Where should we turn when we experience difficulty? I would encourage you to read the Bible. In this old book you will find wisdom that is more relevant than any blog or website you can find on Google. Many times people have picked up the Bible in despair and found hope. Moreover, many have been shocked at how perceptive a book could be to their own situation. You don't read this book; it reads you. Here are just a few Bible verses that I hope will encourage you in whatever difficult circumstance you might be facing.

### *Help with addiction*

So if the Son sets you free, you are truly free.

*John 8:36* (NLT)

Happy is the one who endures testing, because when he has proven to be genuine, he will receive the crown of life that God promised to those who love him.

*James 1:12* (NET)

For everything in the world—the lust of the flesh, the lust of the eyes, and the pride of life—comes not from the Father but from the world.

*1 John 2:16* (NIV)

### *Help with anxiety*

Casting all your anxieties on him, because he cares for you.

*1 Peter 5:7* (ESV)

Therefore I say to you, do not worry about your life, what you will eat or what you will drink; nor about your body, what you will put on. Is not life more than food and the body more than clothing? Look at the birds of the air, for they neither sow nor reap nor gather into barns; yet your heavenly Father feeds them. Are you not of more value than they? Which of you by worrying can add one cubit to his stature? So why do you worry about clothing? Consider the lilies of the field, how they grow: they neither toil nor spin; and yet I say to you that even Solomon in all his glory was not arrayed like one of these.

*Matthew 6:25–29* (NKJV)

### Help with betrayal

A false witness will not go unpunished, nor will a liar escape.

*Proverbs 19:5* (NLT)

For if you forgive others their sins, your heavenly Father will also forgive you. But if you do not forgive others, your Father will not forgive you your sins.

*Matthew 6:14–15* (NET)

### Help with brokenness

Take my yoke upon you and learn from me, for I am gentle and humble in heart, and you will find rest for your souls.

*Matthew 11:29* (NIV)

The LORD is near to the brokenhearted and saves the crushed in spirit.

*Psalm 34:18* (ESV)

Every word of God is pure; He is a shield to those who put their trust in Him.

*Proverbs 30:5* (NKJV)

### Help with contentment

Do not store up for yourselves treasures on earth, where moths and vermin destroy, and where thieves break in and steal. But store up for yourselves treasures in heaven, where moths and vermin do not destroy, and where thieves do not break in and steal. For where your treasure is, there your heart will be also.

*Matthew 6:19–21* (NIV)

Remove falsehood and lies far from me; do not give me poverty or riches, feed me with my allotted portion of bread, lest I become satisfied and act deceptively and say, "Who is the LORD?" Or lest I become poor and steal and demean the name of my God.

*Proverbs 30:8–9* (NET)

Seek the Kingdom of God above all else, and live righteously, and he will give you everything you need.

*Matthew 6:33* (NLT)

But godliness with contentment is great gain, for we brought nothing into the world, and we cannot take anything out of the world. But if we have food and clothing, with these we will be content.

*1 Timothy 6:6–8* (ESV)

### Help with pain

Blessed be the God and Father of our Lord Jesus Christ, the Father of mercies and God of all comfort, who comforts us in all our tribulation, that we may be able to comfort those who are in any trouble, with the comfort with which we ourselves are comforted by God.

*2 Corinthians 1:3–4* (NKJV)

Even though I walk through the darkest valley, I will fear no evil, for you are w; your rod and your staff, they comfort me.

*Psalm 23:4* (NIV)

Blessed are those who mourn, for they will be comforted.

*Matthew 5:4* (NET)

I have told you all this so that you may have peace in me. Here on earth you will have many trials and sorrows. But take heart, because I have overcome the world.

*John 16:33* (NLT)

## *Help with depression*

But God, who comforts the downcast, comforted us.

*2 Corinthians 7:6* (ESV)

Answer me speedily, O LORD; My spirit fails! Do not hide Your face from me, Lest I be like those who go down into the pit. Cause me to hear Your lovingkindness in the morning, For in You do I trust; Cause me to know the way in which I should walk, For I lift up my soul to You.

*Psalm 143:7–8* (NKJV)

The LORD is a refuge for the oppressed, a stronghold in times of trouble.

*Psalm 9:9* (NIV)

Why are you depressed, O my soul? Why are you upset? Wait for God!

*Psalm 43:5* (NET)

## *Help with guilt*

So now there is no condemnation for those who belong to Christ Jesus.

*Romans 8:1* (NLT)

Everyone who calls on the name of the Lord will be saved.

*Romans 10:13* (ESV)

But if we walk in the light as He is in the light, we have fellowship with one another, and the blood of Jesus Christ His Son cleanses us from all sin.

*1 John 1:7* (NKJV)

With it he touched my mouth and said, "See, this has touched your lips; your guilt is taken away and your sin atoned for."

*Isaiah 6:7* (NIV)

### *Help with loneliness*

Even if my father and mother abandoned me, the LORD would take me in.

*Psalm 27:10* (NET)

Don't be afraid, for I am with you. Don't be discouraged, for I am your God. I will strengthen you and help you. I will hold you up with my victorious right hand.

*Isaiah 41:10* (NLT)

Keep your life free from love of money, and be content with what you have, for he has said, "I will never leave you nor forsake you."

*Hebrews 13:5* (ESV)

### *Help with rejection*

Coming to Him as to a living stone, rejected indeed by men, but chosen by God and precious.

*1 Peter 2:4* (NKJV)

For the LORD will not reject his people; he will never forsake his inheritance.

*Psalm 94:14* (NIV)

If God is for us, who can be against us?

*Romans 8:31* (NET)

### *Help with restlessness*

Be still, and know that I am God! I will be honored by every nation. I will be honored throughout the world.

*Psalm 46:10* (NLT)

Be still before the LORD and wait patiently for him; fret not yourself over the one who prospers in his way, over the man who carries out evil devices!

*Psalm 37:7* (ESV)

Come to Me, all you who labor and are heavy laden, and I will give you rest. Take My yoke upon you and learn from Me, for I am gentle and lowly in heart, and you will find rest for your souls. For My yoke is easy and My burden is light.

*Matthew 11:28–30* (NKJV)

Then Jesus said, "Let's go off by ourselves to a quiet place and rest awhile."

*Mark 6:31* (NLT)

It is vain for you to rise early, come home late, and work so hard for your food. Yes, he provides for those whom he loves even when they sleep.

*Psalm 127:2* (NET)

My Presence will go with you, and I will give you rest.

*Exodus 33:14* (NIV)

In peace I will both lie down and sleep; for you alone, O LORD, make me dwell in safety.

*Psalm 4:8* (ESV)

### *Help with protection*

The eternal God is your refuge, and underneath are the everlasting arms.

*Deuteronomy 33:27* (NKJV)

Whoever dwells in the shelter of the Most High will rest in the shadow of the Almighty. I will say of the LORD, "He is my refuge and my fortress, my God, in whom I trust." Surely he will save you from the fowler's snare and from the deadly pestilence. He will cover you with his feathers, and under his wings you will find refuge; his faithfulness will be your shield and rampart. You will not fear the terror of night, nor the arrow that flies by day.

*Psalm 91:1–5* (NIV)

I constantly trust in the LORD; because he is at my right hand, I will not be shaken.

*Psalm 16:8* (NET)

Having hope will give you courage. You will be protected and will rest in safety.

*Job 11:18* (NLT)

He drew me up from the pit of destruction, out of the miry bog, and set my feet upon a rock, making my steps secure.

*Psalm 40:2* (ESV)

For You have been a shelter for me, A strong tower from the enemy. I will abide in Your tabernacle forever; I will trust in the shelter of Your wings.

*Psalm 61:3–4* (NKJV)

God is our refuge and strength, an ever-present help in trouble.

*Psalm 46:1* (NIV)

### Help with shame

Instead of shame, you will get a double portion; instead of humiliation, they will rejoice over the land they receive. Yes, they will possess a double portion in their land and experience lasting joy.

*Isaiah 61:7* (NET)

Because the Sovereign LORD helps me, I will not be disgraced. Therefore, I have set my face like a stone, determined to do his will. And I know that I will not be put to shame.

*Isaiah 50:7* (NLT)

I sought the LORD, and he answered me and delivered me from all my fears. Those who look to him are radiant, and their faces shall never be ashamed.

*Psalm 34:4–5* (ESV)

For the Scripture says, "Whoever believes on Him will not be put to shame."

*Romans 10:11* (NKJV)

Do not be afraid; you will not be put to shame. Do not fear disgrace; you will not be humiliated. You will forget the shame of your youth and remember no more the reproach of your widowhood.

*Isaiah 54:4* (NIV)

## *Help with suicidal feelings*

Why should you die before your time?

*Ecclesiastes 7:17* (ESV)

"For I know the plans I have for you," says the LORD. "They are plans for good and not for disaster, to give you a future and a hope."

*Jeremiah 29:11* (NLT)

For you were bought at a price. Therefore glorify God with your body.

*1 Corinthians 6:20* (NET)

I call heaven and earth as witnesses today against you, that I have set before you life and death, blessing and cursing; therefore choose life, that both you and your descendants may live.

*Deuteronomy 30:19* (NKJV)

So do not throw away your confidence; it will be richly rewarded. You need to persevere so that when you have done the will of God, you will receive what he has promised.

*Hebrews 10:35–36* (NIV)

## *Help with weakness*

But he said to me, "My grace is enough for you, for my power is made perfect in weakness." So then, I will boast most gladly about my weaknesses, so that the power of Christ may reside in me.

*2 Corinthians 12:9* (NET)

This High Priest of ours understands our weaknesses, for he faced all of the same testings we do, yet he did not sin. So let us come boldly to the throne of our gracious God. There we will receive his mercy, and we will find grace to help us when we need it most.

*Hebrews 4:15–16* (NLT)

But he gives more grace. Therefore it says, "God opposes the proud but gives grace to the humble."

*James 4:6* (ESV)

Therefore I take pleasure in infirmities, in reproaches, in needs, in persecutions, in distresses, for Christ's sake. For when I am weak, then I am strong.

*2 Corinthians 12:10* (NKJV)

# What You Need to Know about Spiritual Beings

For centuries there has been a fascination with the spiritual realm. Some people claim to have seen ghosts; others have seen demons; most would agree that this world is getting darker. The Bible does speak of demons, angels, and Satan, but not in the same way many Hollywood movies portray the spiritual realm. It does warn us that there is an enemy who wants to drag us to hell and blind our eyes from seeing the wonderful sacrifice that God prepared for all people by sending His Son Jesus to rescue us.

We all need to be aware of the invisible battle that is happening right now between good and evil; that way, we will know which captain to hide behind, Christ or the devil. The good news is the devil was defeated at the cross when Jesus paid the ransom for our sins. When He rose from the dead, this proved that the powers of death had no hold on Him.

The Bible promises us that at the end of this world Satan will be captured and cast into hell for all eternity. That's why you would be very wise to join the winning side. The King of kings, Jesus Christ, calls you to enlist today. Will you answer His call and march under His name today?

### The devil

Be alert and of sober mind. Your enemy the devil prowls around like a roaring lion looking for someone to devour.

*1 Peter 5:8* (NIV)

So submit to God. But resist the devil and he will flee from you.

*James 4:7* (NET)

These people are . . . deceitful workers who disguise themselves as apostles of Christ. But I am not surprised! Even Satan disguises himself as an angel of light.

*2 Corinthians 11:13–14* (NLT)

Therefore rejoice, O heavens, and you who dwell in them! Woe to the inhabitants of the earth and the sea! For the devil has come down to you, having great wrath, because he knows that he has a short time.

*Revelation 12:12* (NKJV)

We know that everyone who has been born of God does not keep on sinning, but he who was born of God protects him, and the evil one does not touch him. We know that we are from God, and the whole world lies in the power of the evil one.

*1 John 5:18–19* (ESV)

You belong to your father, the devil, and you want to carry out your father's desires. He was a murderer from the beginning, not holding to the truth, for there is no truth in him. When he lies, he speaks his native language, for he is a liar and the father of lies.

*John 8:44* (NIV)

Clothe yourselves with the full armor of God, so that you will be able to stand against the schemes of the devil. For our struggle is not against flesh and blood, but against the rulers, against the powers, against the world rulers of this darkness, against the spiritual forces of evil in the heavens.

*Ephesians 6:11–12* (NET)

Satan, who is the god of this world, has blinded the minds of those who don't believe. They are unable to see the glorious light of the Good News. They don't understand this message about the glory of Christ, who is the exact likeness of God.

*2 Corinthians 4:4* (NLT)

The thief comes only to steal and kill and destroy.

*John 10:10* (ESV)

The devil, who deceived them, was cast into the lake of fire and brimstone where the beast and the false prophet are. And they will be tormented day and night forever and ever.

*Revelation 20:10* (NKJV)

Since the children have flesh and blood, he too shared in their humanity so that by his death he might break the power of him who holds the power of death—that is, the devil.

*Hebrews 2:14* (NIV)

Simon, Simon, Satan has asked to sift each of you like wheat. But I have pleaded in prayer for you, Simon, that your faith should not fail. So when you have repented and turned to me again, strengthen your brothers.

*Luke 22:31–32* (NLT)

## Angels

For He shall give His angels charge over you, to keep you in all your ways.

*Psalm 91:11* (NKJV)

Do not forget to show hospitality to strangers, for by so doing some people have shown hospitality to angels without knowing it.

*Hebrews 13:2* (NIV)

The angel of the LORD camps around the LORD's loyal followers and delivers them.

*Psalm 34:7* (NET)

Praise the LORD, you angels, you mighty ones who carry out his plans, listening for each of his commands.

*Psalm 103:20* (NLT)

Just so, I tell you, there is joy before the angels of God over one sinner who repents.

*Luke 15:10* (ESV)

Take heed that you do not despise one of these little ones, for I say to you that in heaven their angels always see the face of My Father who is in heaven.

*Matthew 18:10* (NKJV)

### Demons

You believe that there is one God. Good! Even the demons believe that—and shudder.

*James 2:19* (NIV)

When an unclean spirit goes out of a person, it passes through waterless places looking for rest but does not find it. Then it says, "I will return to the home I left." When it returns, it finds the house empty, swept clean, and put in order. Then it goes and brings with it seven other spirits more evil than itself, and they go in and live there, so the last state of that person is worse than the first. It will be that way for this evil generation as well!

*Matthew 12:43–45* (NET)

Jesus called his twelve disciples together and gave them authority to cast out evil spirits and to heal every kind of disease and illness.

*Matthew 10:1* (NLT)

Now the Spirit expressly says that in later times some will depart from the faith by devoting themselves to deceitful spirits and teachings of demons.

*1 Timothy 4:1* (ESV)

And the unclean spirits, whenever they saw Him, fell down before Him and cried out, saying, "You are the Son of God."

*Mark 3:11* (NKJV)

No, but the sacrifices of pagans are offered to demons, not to God, and I do not want you to be participants with demons.

*1 Corinthians 10:20* (NIV)

# What You Need to Know about You

God is not a distant grandfather sitting on a cloud, ignoring you. No, the real God cares about you. No one has the right to say, "No one loves me," because God loves you and longs for a relationship with you. That's the message of the cross: that Jesus went to great lengths and suffered unimaginable pain to restore the lost relationship between people and God—lost because of our sin. God listens; God cares; God is always there for any willing person who wants to talk to Him in prayer. Everything you do matters to God, and these Bible verses below prove it!

## *Your birth*

For you formed my inward parts; you knitted me together in my mother's womb. I praise you, for I am fearfully and wonderfully made.

*Psalm 139:13–14* (ESV)

When a woman gives birth, she has distress because her time has come, but when her child is born, she no longer remembers the suffering because of her joy that a human being has been born into the world.

*John 16:21* (NET)

For everything there is a season, a time for every activity under heaven. A time to be born and a time to die. A time to plant and a time to harvest.

*Ecclesiastes 3:1–2* (NLT)

## *Your body*

So God created man in His own image; in the image of God He created him; male and female He created them.

*Genesis 1:27* (NKJV)

The eye is the lamp of the body. If your eyes are healthy, your whole body will be full of light.

*Matthew 6:22 (NIV)*

If there is a natural body, there is also a spiritual body.

*1 Corinthians 15:44 (NET)*

Don't be afraid of those who want to kill your body; they cannot touch your soul. Fear only God, who can destroy both soul and body in hell.

*Matthew 10:28 (NLT)*

## *Your choices*

Choose this day whom you will serve.

*Joshua 24:15 (ESV)*

There is a way that seems right to a man, but its end is the way of death.

*Proverbs 14:12 (NKJV)*

Now all has been heard; here is the conclusion of the matter: Fear God and keep his commandments, for this is the duty of all mankind. For God will bring every deed into judgment, including every hidden thing, whether it is good or evil.

*Ecclesiastes 12:13–14 (NIV)*

Enter through the narrow gate, because the gate is wide and the way is spacious that leads to destruction, and there are many who enter through it. How narrow is the gate and difficult the way that leads to life, and there are few who find it!

*Matthew 7:13–14 (NET)*

## *Your family*

Honor your father and mother. Then you will live a long, full life in the land the LORD your God is giving you.

*Exodus 20:12 (NLT)*

Therefore a man shall leave his father and his mother and hold fast to his wife, and they shall become one flesh.

*Genesis 2:24* (ESV)

He who finds a wife finds a good thing, and obtains favor from the LORD.

*Proverbs 18:22* (NKJV)

## *Your heart*

Create in me a pure heart, O God, and renew a steadfast spirit within me.

*Psalm 51:10* (NIV)

And I will give you a new heart, and I will put a new spirit in you. I will take out your stony, stubborn heart and give you a tender, responsive heart.

*Ezekiel 36:26* (NLT)

Guard your heart with all vigilance, for from it are the sources of life.

*Proverbs 4:23* (NET)

The heart is deceitful above all things, and desperately sick; who can understand it?

*Jeremiah 17:9* (ESV)

Blessed are the pure in heart, for they shall see God.

*Matthew 5:8* (NKJV)

So I strive always to keep my conscience clear before God and man.

*Acts 24:16* (NIV)

## *Your happiness*

Take delight in the LORD, and he will give you your heart's desires.

*Psalm 37:4* (NLT)

Rejoice in the Lord always. Again I say, rejoice!

*Philippians 4:4* (NET)

With joy you will draw water from the wells of salvation.

*Isaiah 12:3* (ESV)

A merry heart does good, like medicine, but a broken spirit dries the bones.

*Proverbs 17:22* (NKJV)

### *Your life*

You do not know about tomorrow. What is your life like? For you are a puff of smoke that appears for a short time and then vanishes.

*James 4:14* (NET)

Jesus spoke to the people once more and said, "I am the light of the world. If you follow me, you won't have to walk in darkness, because you will have the light that leads to life."

*John 8:12* (NLT)

Jesus said to them, "I am the bread of life; whoever comes to me shall not hunger, and whoever believes in me shall never thirst.

*John 6:35* (ESV)

### *Your purpose*

That the name of our Lord Jesus Christ may be glorified in you, and you in Him, according to the grace of our God and the Lord Jesus Christ.

*2 Thessalonians 1:12* (NKJV)

He has shown you, O mortal, what is good. And what does the LORD require of you? To act justly and to love mercy and to walk humbly with your God.

*Micah 6:8* (NIV)

So whether you eat or drink, or whatever you do, do everything for the glory of God.

*1 Corinthians 10:31* (NET)

## *Your past*

Don't long for "the good old days." This is not wise.

*Ecclesiastes 7:10* (NLT)

Remember not the former things, nor consider the things of old. Behold, I am doing a new thing; now it springs forth, do you not perceive it? I will make a way in the wilderness and rivers in the desert.

*Isaiah 43:18–19* (ESV)

Brothers, I do not consider that I have made it my own. But one thing I do: forgetting what lies behind and straining forward to what lies ahead, 14 I press on toward the goal for the prize of the upward call of God in Christ Jesus.

*Philippians 3:13–14* (ESV)

For I will forgive their wickedness and will remember their sins no more.

*Hebrews 8:12* (NIV)

And the one seated on the throne said: "Look! I am making all things new!"

*Revelation 21:5* (NET)

## *Your soul*

Then the LORD God formed the man from the dust of the ground. He breathed the breath of life into the man's nostrils, and the man became a living person [soul].

*Genesis 2:7* (NLT)

You shall love the LORD your God with all your heart and with all your soul and with all your might.

*Deuteronomy 6:5* (ESV)

Behold, all souls are Mine; the soul of the father as well as the soul of the son is Mine; the soul who sins shall die.

*Ezekiel 18:4* (NKJV)

He refreshes my soul. He guides me along the right paths for his name's sake.

*Psalm 23:3* (NIV)

Why are you depressed, O my soul? Why are you upset? Wait for God! For I will again give thanks to my God for his saving intervention.

*Psalm 43:5* (NET)

For you will not leave my soul among the dead or allow your holy one to rot in the grave.

*Psalm 16:10* (NLT)

### Your time

So teach us to number our days that we may get a heart of wisdom.

*Psalm 90:12* (ESV)

Redeeming the time, because the days are evil.

*Ephesians 5:16* (NKJV)

A person plans his course, but the LORD directs his steps.

*Proverbs 16:9* (NET)

My times are in your hands.

*Psalm 31:15* (NIV)

Yet God has made everything beautiful for its own time. He has planted eternity in the human heart, but even so, people cannot see the whole scope of God's work from beginning to end.

*Ecclesiastes 3:11* (NLT)

# Have Any Bible Prophecies Come True?

People often ask for evidence that the Bible is reliable and trustworthy. I believe the Bible itself is the evidence it is reliable.

Hear me out! Suppose you knew a book that would make historical claims—and we're not talking about small claims like it will snow in May—but huge claims like a man would be born of a virgin and rise from the dead. Imagine if such a book existed and made these predictions, then thousands of years later these things came true in a real person, in a real place, at a real time.

That's exactly how things unfolded in the Bible. In the Old Testament there were very precise predictions made about the Savior Jesus and in the New Testament we read eyewitness accounts of these predictions coming to pass. Moreover, you can research other sources outside of the Bible that confirm these events were historically accurate. Here is a fraction of the prophecies that came true surrounding the person of Jesus Christ.

(Please note: The dates that precede the Scripture verses are the approximate dates the verses were written. All the prophecies were fulfilled in the first century AD.)

## *The Christ will be born of a virgin*

*Prediction (740 BC):*
Look! The virgin will conceive a child! She will give birth to a son and will call him Immanuel (which means 'God is with us').

*Isaiah 7:14* (NLT)

*What happened?*

Now the birth of Jesus Christ was as follows: After His mother Mary was betrothed to Joseph, before they came together, she was found with child of the Holy Spirit.

*Matthew 1:18* (NKJV)


## *The Christ will be born in Bethlehem*

*Prediction (700 BC):*

But you, Bethlehem Ephrathah, though you are small among the clans of Judah, out of you will come for me one who will be ruler over Israel, whose origins are from of old, from ancient times.

*Micah 5:2* (NIV)

*What happened?*

After Jesus was born in Bethlehem in Judea, in the time of King Herod, wise men from the East came to Jerusalem.

*Matthew 2:1* (NET)


## *The Christ will enter Jerusalem on a donkey*

*Prediction (518 BC):*

Rejoice, O people of Zion! Shout in triumph, O people of Jerusalem! Look, your king is coming to you. He is righteous and victorious, yet he is humble, riding on a donkey—riding on a donkey's colt.

*Zechariah 9:9* (NLT)

*What happened?*

And Jesus found a young donkey and sat on it, just as it is written.

*John 12:14* (ESV)

## The Christ will be betrayed by a close friend

*Prediction (1010–930 BC):*
Even my own familiar friend in whom I trusted, who ate my bread, has lifted up his heel against me.

*Psalm 41:9* (NKJV)

*What happened?*
Jesus replied, "The one who has dipped his hand into the bowl with me will betray me."

*Matthew 26:23* (NIV)

## The Christ will be sold for thirty pieces of silver

*Prediction (518 BC):*
Then I said to them, "If it seems good to you, pay me my wages, but if not, forget it." So they weighed out my payment—thirty pieces of silver.

*Zechariah 11:12* (NET)

*What happened?*
And [Judas] asked, "How much will you pay me to betray Jesus to you?" And they gave him thirty pieces of silver.

*Matthew 26:15* (NLT)

## The Christ's garments would be divided

*Prediction (1010–930 BC):*
They divide my garments among them, and for my clothing they cast lots.

*Psalm 22:18* (ESV)

*What happened?*
And when they crucified Him, they divided His garments, casting lots for them to determine what every man should take.

*Mark 15:24* (NKJV)

## The Christ will be struck and spat on

*Prediction (740 BC):*

I offered my back to those who beat me, my cheeks to those who pulled out my beard; I did not hide my face from mocking and spitting.

*Isaiah 50:6 (NIV)*

*What happened?*

Then some began to spit on him, and to blindfold him, and to strike him with their fists, saying, "Prophesy!" The guards also took him and beat him.

*Mark 14:65 (NET)*

## The Christ will have nails in his hands and feet

*Prediction (1010–930 BC):*

My enemies surround me like a pack of dogs; an evil gang closes in on me. They have pierced my hands and feet.

*Psalm 22:16 (NLT)*

*What happened?*

So the other disciples told him, "We have seen the Lord." But he said to them, "Unless I see in his hands the mark of the nails, and place my finger into the mark of the nails, and place my hand into his side, I will never believe." Eight days later, his disciples were inside again, and Thomas was with them. Although the doors were locked, Jesus came and stood among them and said, "Peace be with you." Then he said to Thomas, "Put your finger here, and see my hands; and put out your hand, and place it in my side. Do not disbelieve, but believe."

*John 20:25–27 (ESV)*

## The Christ will be buried by a rich man

*Prediction (740 BC):*

And they made His grave with the wicked—but with the rich at His death, because He had done no violence, nor was any deceit in His mouth.

*Isaiah 53:9* (NKJV)

*What happened?*

As evening approached, there came a rich man from Arimathea, named Joseph, who had himself become a disciple of Jesus. Going to Pilate, he asked for Jesus' body, and Pilate ordered that it be given to him. Joseph took the body, wrapped it in a clean linen cloth, and placed it in his own new tomb that he had cut out of the rock. He rolled a big stone in front of the entrance to the tomb and went away.

*Matthew 27:57–60* (NIV)


## The Christ will rise again

*Prediction (1010–930 BC):*

For you will not leave my soul among the dead or allow your holy one to rot in the grave.

*Psalm 16:10* (NLT)

*What happened?*

The women were terribly frightened and bowed their faces to the ground, but the men said to them, "Why do you look for the living among the dead? He is not here, but has been raised! Remember how he told you, while he was still in Galilee, that the Son of Man must be delivered into the hands of sinful men, and be crucified, and on the third day rise again."

*Luke 24:5–7* (NET)

# What Will Happen in the Future?

Movie producers and book publishers both know that "end of the world stories" are big business. Why? Because, as human beings, we are fascinated by the unknown and what will happen to us in the future. Every generation has its own ideas and conspiracy theories, but what does the Bible say will happen? One thing is certain: Jesus Christ is coming, and the Bible warns us to be ready for that day. All those who love Christ and have received Him as Lord will spend eternity with Him in paradise. All those who have rejected Jesus (refused to let Him wash away their sins) will receive eternal consequences for their rebellion, because they would rather live in darkness than in the light.

But there is one event that is also certain and may happen before Jesus returns—your death. Every second, dozens of people are thrust into eternity and stand before Jesus. Those people will either be excited to see the One they love or they will feel terror, seeing the One they ignored.

Everyone these days has a robust plan for the future. They have a pension and life insurance; most have already written a will. Some even know who's arranging the flowers at their funeral! But how many have prepared for eternity? Have you considered where your soul will live—not for years, but forever? Come to Christ today—the door is open, and the One who holds it open has kind hands, hands that you can trust with your future.

### Death is coming

For the wages of sin is death, but the free gift of God is eternal life in Christ Jesus our Lord.

*Romans 6:23* (esv)

His spirit departs, he returns to his earth; in that very day his plans perish.

*Psalm 146:4* (NKJV)

Just as people are destined to die once, and after that to face judgment.

*Hebrews 9:27* (NIV)

## *Heaven is coming (for those who love Christ)*

He will wipe away every tear from their eyes, and death will not exist any more—or mourning, or crying, or pain, for the former things have ceased to exist.

*Revelation 21:4* (NET)

There is more than enough room in my Father's home. If this were not so, would I have told you that I am going to prepare a place for you?

*John 14:2* (NLT)

But, as it is written, "What no eye has seen, nor ear heard, nor the heart of man imagined, what God has prepared for those who love him."

*1 Corinthians 2:9* (ESV)

Do not lay up for yourselves treasures on earth, where moth and rust destroy and where thieves break in and steal, but lay up for yourselves treasures in heaven, where neither moth nor rust destroys and where thieves do not break in and steal. For where your treasure is, there your heart will be also.

*Matthew 6:19–21* (ESV)

For here we have no continuing city, but we seek the one to come.

*Hebrews 13:14* (NKJV)

### Hell is coming (for those who reject Christ)

But the cowardly, the unbelieving, the vile, the murderers, the sexually immoral, those who practice magic arts, the idolaters and all liars—they will be consigned to the fiery lake of burning sulfur. This is the second death.

*Revelation 21:8* (NIV)

And these will depart into eternal punishment, but the righteous into eternal life.

*Matthew 25:46* (NET)

Then the King will turn to those on the left and say, "Away with you, you cursed ones, into the eternal fire prepared for the devil and his demons."

*Matthew 25:41* (NLT)

And they shall go out and look on the dead bodies of the men who have rebelled against me. For their worm shall not die, their fire shall not be quenched, and they shall be an abhorrence to all flesh.

*Isaiah 66:24* (ESV)

And cast them into the furnace of fire. There will be wailing and gnashing of teeth.

*Matthew 13:50* (NKJV)

### The end is coming

Now, brothers and sisters, about times and dates we do not need to write to you, for you know very well that the day of the Lord will come like a thief in the night. While people are saying, "Peace and safety," destruction will come on them suddenly, as labor pains on a pregnant woman, and they will not escape. But you, brothers and sisters, are not in darkness so that this day should surprise you like a thief. You are all children of the light and children of the day. We do not belong to the night or to the darkness.

*1 Thessalonians 5:1–5* (NIV)

But understand this, that in the last days difficult times will come. For people will be lovers of themselves, lovers of money, boastful, arrogant, blasphemers, disobedient to parents, ungrateful, unholy, unloving, irreconcilable, slanderers, without self-control, savage, opposed to what is good, treacherous, reckless, conceited, loving pleasure rather than loving God. They will maintain the outward appearance of religion but will have repudiated its power. So avoid people like these.

*2 Timothy 3:1–5* (NET)

Now the Holy Spirit tells us clearly that in the last times some will turn away from the true faith; they will follow deceptive spirits and teachings that come from demons.

*1 Timothy 4:1* (NLT)

And you will hear of wars and rumors of wars. See that you are not alarmed, for this must take place, but the end is not yet. For nation will rise against nation, and kingdom against kingdom, and there will be famines and earthquakes in various places.

*Matthew 24:6–7* (ESV)

### Jesus is coming

But the day of the Lord will come as a thief in the night, in which the heavens will pass away with a great noise, and the elements will melt with fervent heat; both the earth and the works that are in it will be burned up.

*2 Peter 3:10* (NKJV)

And if I go and prepare a place for you, I will come back and take you to be with me that you also may be where I am.

*John 14:3* (NIV)

As they were still staring into the sky while he was going, suddenly two men in white clothing stood near them and said, "Men of Galilee, why do you stand here looking up into the sky? This same Jesus who has been taken up from you into heaven will come back in the same way you saw him go into heaven."

*Acts 1:10–11* (NET)

Watch out! Don't let your hearts be dulled by carousing and drunkenness, and by the worries of this life. Don't let that day catch you unaware, like a trap. For that day will come upon everyone living on the earth. Keep alert at all times. And pray that you might be strong enough to escape these coming horrors and stand before the Son of Man.

*Luke 21:34–36* (NLT)

"Behold, I am coming soon, bringing my recompense with me, to repay each one for what he has done.

*Revelation 22:12* (ESV)

# Now that I'm a Christian, How Do I Nurture My Faith?-

If you are already a Christian (perhaps even as a result of reading these Bible verses), what should you do? The best advice I can give you is the advice I was given when I first committed my life to Jesus. Every new believer in Christ should do five things:

1. **Read the Bible every day.** God speaks to us directly through His Word, the Bible. If we want to know more about God and grow in our faith, we need to spend time being taught by the Bible. Christians call this "feeding on the Word." Just like a man who doesn't eat regularly will become malnourished, so a man who doesn't feed on the Bible will starve spiritually.

2. **Pray daily.** If reading the Bible is likened to eating food, prayer should be likened to oxygen. Prayer is the Christian's greatest privilege. The God of heaven who created the universe loves to hear His children talk to Him. Without prayer, the Christian will feel distant from God and be more susceptible to falling back into sin. Imagine if I did not speak to my wife for two weeks—would that be a healthy marriage? No! So we must also carve out time every day to have fellowship and conversation with our God. Tell Him how much you love Him, confess your failures of that day to Him, thank Him for the food you eat and the clothes you wear, and bring any needs or concerns before Him, for He delights to care for His children.

3. **Spend time with other Christians.** The Christian life is not for lone rangers, it's a team effort! Our first house was heated with coal; when all the coals were stacked close together, the furnace emitted a glorious heat. However, if you took one coal out of the furnace and isolated

it, it quickly went out—until you placed it back with the other coals. We are like coal; we burn better with other Christians. The church is God's mission force, and together we seek to reach this broken world with the message that saved us; at the same time, we try to build each other up. When we fall into a ditch (and Christians do mess up), we need others to lift us out. That's why a local church is so vital; we need regular contact with Christian friends who understand the unusual battles the believer will face.

4. **Get baptized.** Baptism is important because Jesus commands us to be baptized, and we want to do everything we can to obey our Lord. When a Christian gets baptized, it sends out a powerful message to the world. As they enter beneath the waters, the old person is being buried with Christ, just like Jesus was buried in the tomb. When a Christian is raised out of the water, it's a sign that the new person is here. They are alive with Christ; they have risen with Him to newness of life, just as Jesus rose from the grave. What a beautiful message this sends out to our friends and family! That's why baptism is crucial.

5. **Share your testimony.** God has changed you and saved you, not for you to keep the message to yourself, but to share your story with others so that they might find Jesus too. What would you think of a man who had a cure for one of the most deadly diseases in the world but kept it to himself? You'd say that man is selfish, perhaps even hateful! But we as Christians have something even more precious than an earthly cure for a disease; we have the cure for death—a medicine that leads to eternal life! We know about the Savior who saves souls and empties graves, and that's why we must tell others about Him, and how He has impacted our lives. In addition, the wonderful thing about sharing our testimony is that

it makes us feel good to remind ourselves where we've been and how God has transformed us. The more we talk about Jesus, the more He will mean to us because expression leads to impression!

I hope the verses below confirm how important it is to nurture your newfound faith in Jesus Christ.


## *What should I remember?*

And this is the testimony: that God has given us eternal life, and this life is in His Son. He who has the Son has life; he who does not have the Son of God does not have life. These things I have written to you who believe in the name of the Son of God, that you may know that you have eternal life, and that you may continue to believe in the name of the Son of God.

*1 John 5:11–13* (NKJV)

Therefore, since we have been justified through faith, we have peace with God through our Lord Jesus Christ.

*Romans 5:1* (NIV)

And my God will supply your every need according to his glorious riches in Christ Jesus.

*Philippians 4:19* (NET)

And because of his glory and excellence, he has given us great and precious promises. These are the promises that enable you to share his divine nature and escape the world's corruption caused by human desires.

*2 Peter 1:4* (NLT)

And we know that for those who love God all things work together for good, for those who are called according to his purpose.

*Romans 8:28* (ESV)

And the Lord, He is the One who goes before you. He will be with you, He will not leave you nor forsake you; do not fear nor be dismayed.

*Deuteronomy 31:8* (NKJV)

## *How should I pray?*

When you pray, say: "Father, hallowed be your name. Your kingdom come. Give us each day our daily bread, and forgive us our sins, for we ourselves forgive everyone who is indebted to us. And lead us not into temptation."

*Luke 11:2–4* (ESV)

Until now you have not asked for anything in my name. Ask and you will receive, and your joy will be complete.

*John 16:24* (NIV)

Constantly pray.

*1 Thessalonians 5:17* (NET)

But when you pray, go away by yourself, shut the door behind you, and pray to your Father in private. Then your Father, who sees everything, will reward you.

*Matthew 6:6* (NLT)

Therefore, confess your sins to one another and pray for one another, that you may be healed. The prayer of a righteous person has great power as it is working.

*James 5:16* (ESV)

So I say to you, ask, and it will be given to you; seek, and you will find; knock, and it will be opened to you.

*Luke 11:9* (NKJV)

Call to me and I will answer you and tell you great and unsearchable things you do not know.

*Jeremiah 33:3* (NIV)

Stay awake and pray that you will not fall into temptation. The spirit is willing, but the flesh is weak.

*Matthew 26:41* (NET)

Don't make rash promises, and don't be hasty in bringing matters before God. After all, God is in heaven, and you are here on earth. So let your words be few.

*Ecclesiastes 5:2* (NLT)

### *Is reading the Bible important?*

Do your best to present yourself to God as one approved, a worker who has no need to be ashamed, rightly handling the word of truth.

*2 Timothy 2:15* (ESV)

As newborn babes, desire the pure milk of the word, that you may grow thereby.

*1 Peter 2:2* (NKJV)

How can a young person stay on the path of purity? By living according to your word.

*Psalm 119:9* (NIV)

Your instructions are a doorway through which light shines. They give insight to the untrained.

*Psalm 119:130* (NET)

I have hidden your word in my heart, that I might not sin against you.

*Psalm 119:11* (NLT)

Blessed is the man who walks not in the counsel of the wicked, nor stands in the way of sinners, nor sits in the seat of scoffers; but his delight is in the law of the LORD, and on his law he meditates day and night. He is like a tree planted by streams of water that yields its fruit in its season, and its leaf does not wither. In all that he does, he prospers.

*Psalm 1:1–3* (ESV)

## Should I go to church?

And let us consider one another in order to stir up love and good works, not forsaking the assembling of ourselves together, as is the manner of some, but exhorting one another, and so much the more as you see the Day approaching.

*Hebrews 10:24–25* (NKJV)

I rejoiced with those who said to me, "Let us go to the house of the LORD."

*Psalm 122:1* (NIV)

For where two or three are assembled in my name, I am there among them.

*Matthew 18:20* (NET)

However, the Most High doesn't live in temples made by human hands.

*Acts 7:48* (NLT)

## Why is baptism important?

And Peter said to them, "Repent and be baptized every one of you in the name of Jesus Christ for the forgiveness of your sins, and you will receive the gift of the Holy Spirit.

*Acts 2:38* (ESV)

And now why are you waiting? Arise and be baptized, and wash away your sins, calling on the name of the Lord.

*Acts 22:16* (NKJV)

Whoever believes and is baptized will be saved, but whoever does not believe will be condemned.

*Mark 16:16* (NIV)

And this prefigured baptism, which now saves you—not the washing off of physical dirt but the pledge of a good conscience to God—through the resurrection of Jesus Christ.

*1 Peter 3:21* (NET)

For we died and were buried with Christ by baptism. And just as Christ was raised from the dead by the glorious power of the Father, now we also may live new lives.

*Romans 6:4* (NLT)

Having been buried with him in baptism, in which you were also raised with him through faith in the powerful working of God, who raised him from the dead.

*Colossians 2:12* (ESV)

### *How can I serve God as a Christian?*

And He said to them, "Go into all the world and preach the gospel to every creature."

*Mark 16:15* (NKJV)

He commanded us to preach to the people and to testify that he is the one whom God appointed as judge of the living and the dead.

*Acts 10:42* (NIV)

But the wise will shine like the brightness of the heavenly expanse. And those bringing many to righteousness will be like the stars forever and ever.

*Daniel 12:3* (NET)

God has given each of you a gift from his great variety of spiritual gifts. Use them well to serve one another.

*1 Peter 4:10* (NLT)

Show hospitality to one another without grumbling. As each has received a gift, use it to serve one another, as good stewards of God's varied grace: whoever speaks, as one who speaks oracles of God; whoever serves, as one who serves by the strength that God supplies—in order that in everything God may be glorified through Jesus Christ. To him belong glory and dominion forever and ever. Amen.

*1 Peter 4:9–11* (ESV)

For you, brethren, have been called to liberty; only do not use liberty as an opportunity for the flesh, but through love serve one another.

*Galatians 5:13* (NKJV)

Whatever you do, work at it with all your heart, as working for the Lord, not for human masters, since you know that you will receive an inheritance from the Lord as a reward. It is the Lord Christ you are serving.

*Colossians 3:23–24* (NIV)

You must actively help the hungry and feed the oppressed. Then your light will dispel the darkness, and your darkness will be transformed into noonday.

*Isaiah 58:10* (NET)

Then the King will say to those on his right, "Come, you who are blessed by my Father, inherit the Kingdom prepared for you from the creation of the world. For I was hungry, and you fed me. I was thirsty, and you gave me a drink. I was a stranger, and you invited me into your home. I was naked, and you gave me clothing. I was sick, and you cared for me. I was in prison, and you visited me."

Then these righteous ones will reply, "Lord, when did we ever see you hungry and feed you? Or thirsty and give you something to drink? Or a stranger and show you hospitality? Or naked and give you clothing? When did we ever see you sick or in prison and visit you?"

And the King will say, "I tell you the truth, when you did it to one of the least of these my brothers and sisters, you were doing it to me!"

*Matthew 25:34–40* (NLT)

And he sat down and called the twelve. And he said to them, "If anyone would be first, he must be last of all and servant of all."

*Mark 9:35* (ESV)

# Common Excuses

Now that you've read this far, you've heard the gospel (good news) and you know what you need to do, but maybe you're still unsure. Everyone has an excuse for not bowing their knee to Christ, but I hope you will see the urgency in making this decision and that you will not treat the destination of your eternal soul lightly. Here are some common excuses men and women often make that the Bible easily answers.

### Aren't we all going to heaven anyway?

The wicked shall be turned into hell, and all the nations that forget God.

*Psalm 9:17* (NKJV)

Anyone whose name was not found written in the book of life was thrown into the lake of fire.

*Revelation 20:15* (NIV)

Such is the destiny of all who forget God; the hope of the godless perishes.

*Job 8:13* (NET)

You can enter God's Kingdom only through the narrow gate. The highway to hell is broad, and its gate is wide for the many who choose that way. But the gateway to life is very narrow and the road is difficult, and only a few ever find it.

*Matthew 7:13–14* (NLT)

### What about other religions?

And there is salvation in no one else, for there is no other name under heaven given among men by which we must be saved.

*Acts 4:12* (ESV)

Therefore I said to you that you will die in your sins; for if you do not believe that I am He, you will die in your sins.

*John 8:24* (NKJV)

Anyone who does not enter the sheep pen by the gate, but climbs in by some other way, is a thief and a robber. The one who enters by the gate is the shepherd of the sheep. The gatekeeper opens the gate for him, and the sheep listen to his voice. He calls his own sheep by name and leads them out. When he has brought out all his own, he goes on ahead of them, and his sheep follow him because they know his voice.

*John 10:1–4* (NIV)

### *I'm a good person.*

For all have sinned and fall short of the glory of God

*Romans 3:23* (NET)

If we claim we have no sin, we are only fooling ourselves and not living in the truth.

*1 John 1:8* (NLT)

There is none who understands; there is none who seeks after God.

*Romans 3:11* (NKJV)

### *I've got other things to focus on right now.*

What good is it for someone to gain the whole world, yet forfeit their soul?

*Mark 8:36* (NIV)

But one after another they all began to make excuses. The first said to him, "I have bought a field, and I must go out and see it. Please excuse me." Another said, "I have bought five yoke of oxen, and I am going out to examine them. Please excuse me." Another said, "I just got married, and I cannot come."

*Luke 14:18–20* (NET)

Therefore you have no excuse, O man.

*Romans 2:1* (ESV)

## Is Christianity going to kill my fun?

[Jesus said] "I am the gate. Those who come in through me will be saved. . . . My purpose is to give them a rich and satisfying life."

*John 10:9–10* (NLT)

Nothing is better for a man than that he should eat and drink, and that his soul should enjoy good in his labor. This also, I saw, was from the hand of God. For who can eat, or who can have enjoyment, more than I?

*Ecclesiastes 2:24–25* (NKJV)

Command those who are rich in this present world not to be arrogant nor to put their hope in wealth, which is so uncertain, but to put their hope in God, who richly provides us with everything for our enjoyment.

*1 Timothy 6:17* (NIV)

You lead me in the path of life. I experience absolute joy in your presence; you always give me sheer delight.

*Psalm 16:11* (NET)

He [Moses] chose to share the oppression of God's people instead of enjoying the fleeting pleasures of sin.

*Hebrews 11:25* (NLT)

## Is this really God, or just an emotional phase?

You did not choose me, but I chose you and appointed you that you should go and bear fruit and that your fruit should abide, so that whatever you ask the Father in my name, he may give it to you.

*John 15:16* (ESV)

Just as He chose us in Him before the foundation of the world, that we should be holy and without blame before Him in love, having predestined us to adoption as sons by Jesus Christ to Himself, according to the good pleasure of His will.

*Ephesians 1:4–5* (NKJV)

He has saved us and called us to a holy life—not because of anything we have done but because of his own purpose and grace. This grace was given us in Christ Jesus before the beginning of time.

*2 Timothy 1:9* (NIV)

### Maybe I'll respond to Christ later.

And do this because we know the time, that it is already the hour for us to awake from sleep, for our salvation is now nearer than when we became believers.

*Romans 13:11* (NET)

I am coming soon. Hold on to what you have, so that no one will take away your crown.

*Revelation 3:11* (NLT)

For he says, "In a favorable time I listened to you, and in a day of salvation I have helped you." Behold, now is the favorable time; behold, now is the day of salvation.

*2 Corinthians 6:2* (ESV)

Repent, for the kingdom of heaven is at hand!

*Matthew 3:2* (NKJV)

Seek the LORD while he may be found; call on him while he is near.

*Isaiah 55:6* (NIV)

**PUBLICATIONS**

Fort Washington, PA 19034

This book is published by CLC Publications, an outreach of CLC Ministries International. The purpose of CLC is to make evangelical Christian literature available to all nations so that people may come to faith and maturity in the Lord Jesus Christ. We hope this book has been life changing and has enriched your walk with God through the work of the Holy Spirit. If you would like to know more about CLC, we invite you to visit our website:

**www.clcusa.org**

To know more about the remarkable story of the founding of CLC International we encourage you to read

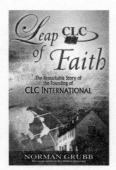

**LEAP OF FAITH**

*Norman Grubb*

Paperback
Size 5¼ x 8, Pages 249
ISBN: 978-0-87508-650-7 - $11.99
ISBN (*e-book*): 978-1-61958-055-8 - $9.99

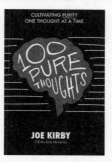

## *100 PURE THOUGHTS*
### *Cultivating Purity One Thought at a Time*

Joe Kirby

*From Joe Kirby of Off the Kirb Ministries, with over 800,000 subscribers to his popular YouTube channel, comes a devotional for believers wrestling with pornography, lust, and other sexual sins.*

Each "thought" begins with a Bible text which is applied to sexual sin and how to overcome it. There is also so much word imagery since every person's mind is a picture gallery. Sexual sin is a visual sin, so therefore the best way to combat it is with visual descriptions and personal stories to engage the reader.

But above all, this devotional is gospel-focused. Only Jesus can break these chains. Sometimes He does so gently, with grace; other times He shatters the fetters with the words of His mouth. These 100 thoughts are a balance of stern warnings and compassionate reminders of who the Son of God is.

Paperback
Size 4¹/₄ x 7, 128 Pages
ISBN: 978-1-61958-346-7
ISBN (*e-book*): 978-1-61958-347-4